Quick & Easy
Tasty Vegetarian

p

Contents

Introduction

Fruit and vegetables, which are natural sources of vitamins and minerals, form the basis of a huge variety of meals. These foods offer a multitude of different colours and variety of tastes which, when combined with herbs and spices, create an explosion of sumptuous flavours. Due to the enormous variety of foods available on the vegetarian menu, vegetarian cooking is now extremely popular with meat-eaters, vegetarians and vegans alike. Tasty Vegetarian has combined the most traditional vegetarian dishes with new recipes which together offer some unique and exciting flavours and textures. From pâtés or bhajis as starters, stuffed vegetables and pasta as main courses, to delicious chocolate fudge pudding or butterscotch melts for desserts, this collection of recipes covers all areas of vegetarian cuisine.

Tasty Vegetarian Food

Vegetarian food has come a long way since the nut cutlet! Its growing popularity is due, at least in part, to

the diverse range of influences – from Asia and North Africa, to Italy and Mexico – which have introduced to us a whole new range of exciting ingredients enabling us to make delicious recipes from around the world.

A wide variety of exotic foods can now easily be obtained in local supermarkets. These offer novel textures and flavours making vegetarian cooking more interesting than ever. Try Kashmiri Spinach or a Middle Eastern Salad or why not enjoy a delicious Spanish Tortilla accompanied by Sidekick Vegetables.

Healthy Eating

Many people turn to vegetarian food because it is so healthy. Fruit and vegetables are naturally fat-free and provide plenty of fibre, carbohydrates, vitamins and minerals. Each particular food has a different nutritional benefit and this should be kept in mind when combining various ingredients to ensure a balanced diet.

In varying degrees, fruit and vegetables contain calcium, iron and phosphorous, all of which are important for healthy living. Furthermore, fruit and vegetables are great sources of vitamins. Vitamin A is found in green, yellow and orange vegetables, and

particularly in carrots. Leafy vegetables are an excellent source of vitamin E. Vitamin C is present in many 'fruit vegetables', such as peppers and tomatoes, and may also be found in the roots and leaves of others. Vegetarians should ensure that sufficient levels of protein are maintained in their diets. This is not difficult however, as vegetables can be eaten with pulses or legumes which offer natural sources of protein.

Pulses

Pulses are extremely important to a vegetarian diet and can be found in many forms; from lentils and haricot (navy) beans, to kidney beans and split peas. The nutritional benefits of legumes include high levels of carbohydrates, vitamins – especially vitamin B – and notably iron, which is especially important for women and the elderly. Each of the different pulses gives a different texture to your dish and all can be combined with a rich variety of flavours.

World wide, local gastronomies have influenced the methods of preparing, cooking and serving different legumes enormously. From Massachusetts, the home of the baked bean, to Mexico, and the ubiquitous frijoles or refried beans, to the tasty lentil dhal of India, each region has found an innovative way of spicing up their food.

Eating meals which combine pulses with grains ensures you achieve the complete daily protein required in a healthy diet, so, for example, it is an excellent idea to mop up a lentil soup with tasty wholewheat bread. Recipes have been included in *Tasty Vegetarian* which show you how to combine different food groups to create a variety of flavoursome dishes. Choose from Deep South Rice & Beans, Spiced Rice & Lentils or Moroccan Salad, among others, for a completely balanced meal.

Choosing and Cooking Vegetables

With such a huge variety of vegetables on the market, it is important to choose and cook them in the correct way. When purchasing vegetables make sure that they are neither damaged nor bruised. Leafy vegetables should look green, not yellow, and the leaves should not be slimy or wilting. Root vegetables should be firm with a dull and dry appearance. Fruit should have taut, shiny skins and be firm to the touch.

Preparing vegetables incorrectly can lead to a leaching of vitamins and loss of all-important nutrients. Many vegetables can be eaten raw but cooking often enhances the flavour and changes their texture. There are many different ways they can be prepared, some of which do not require fat. Grilling and barbecuing leaves the food with a crisp outer coating whilst maintaining moist and tender interiors; braising and stewing involve cooking the dish very slowly using liquids — often the natural juices of the ingredients — resulting in tender vegetables which retain all their nutrients, flavours and aromas; boiling and poaching do not use any fat but can lead to loss of essential food groups to the cooking water which is discarded.

If you do boil your vegetables, try to keep cooking times as short as possible to limit the extraction of essential vitamins. And remember, the cooking water can be used afterwards to make soups and sauces as it will be full of flavour and nutrients. Steaming is a healthier alternative to boiling as less water comes into contact with the food. Instead of conventional frying, try stir-frying in a wok as this requires minimal fat and helps retain the goodness and colour of the ingredients.

Cooking Vegetarian for the First Time

For those who have decided to convert to vegetarianism and are cooking meat-free food for the first time there are several ingredients that should be avoided. In particular, gelatine, a protein used to thicken foods, is used in many puddings, however it is made from collagen so a vegetarian substitute should be used instead. Also, many cheeses are made with animal derivatives: strict vegetarians should buy those that have been certified by the Vegetarian Society and have a green 'V' on the label. Vegetarian cheeses are made with rennets of non-animal origin, using microbial or fungal enzymes. When buying pre-packaged ingredients, in particular sweet foods such as biscuits, always check the ingredients to see if animal fats have been used. You should also be aware that some condiments, such as Worcestershire Sauce which is made using anchovies, may contain animal products.

KEY	
	Simplicity level 1 – 3 (1 easiest, 3 slightly harder)
	Preparation time
	Cooking time

Vegetable & Corn Chowder

This is a really filling soup, which should be served before a light main course. It is easy to prepare and filled with flavour.

NUTRITIONAL INFORMATION

Calories	378	Sugars	........20g
Protein	........16g	Fat	..........13g
Carbohydrate	...52g	Saturates	.......6g

 15 MINS   30 MINS

SERVES 4

I N G R E D I E N T S

1 tbsp vegetable oil

1 red onion, diced

1 red pepper, seeded and diced

3 garlic cloves, crushed

1 large potato, diced

2 tbsp plain flour

600 ml/1 pint milk

300 ml/½ pint vegetable stock

50 g/1¾ oz broccoli florets

300 g/10½ oz canned sweetcorn, drained

75 g/2¾ oz Cheddar cheese, grated

salt and pepper

1 tbsp chopped coriander, to garnish

COOK'S TIP

Vegetarian cheeses are made with rennets of non-animal origin, using microbial or fungal enzymes.

1 Heat the oil in a large saucepan. Add the onion, pepper, garlic and potato and sauté over a low heat, stirring frequently, for 2–3 minutes.

2 Stir in the flour and cook, stirring for 30 seconds. Gradually stir in the milk and stock.

3 Add the broccoli and sweetcorn. Bring the mixture to the boil, stirring constantly, then reduce the heat and simmer for about 20 minutes, or until all the vegetables are tender.

4 Stir in 50 g/1¾ oz of the cheese until it melts.

5 Season and spoon the chowder into a warm soup tureen. Garnish with the remaining cheese and the coriander and serve.

Pumpkin Soup

This is an American classic that has now become popular worldwide. When pumpkin is out of season use butternut squash in its place.

NUTRITIONAL INFORMATION

Calories 112	Sugars 7g
Protein 4g	Fat 7g
Carbohydrate 8g	Saturates 2g

 10 MINS   30 MINS

SERVES 6

INGREDIENTS

about 1 kg/2 lb 4 oz pumpkin

40 g/1½ oz butter or margarine

1 onion, sliced thinly

1 garlic clove, crushed

900 ml/1½ pints vegetable stock

½ tsp ground ginger

1 tbsp lemon juice

3–4 thinly pared strips of orange rind (optional)

1–2 bay leaves or 1 bouquet garni

300 ml/½ pint milk

salt and pepper

TO GARNISH

4–6 tablespoons single or double cream, natural yogurt or fromage frais

snipped chives

1 Peel the pumpkin, remove the seeds and then cut the flesh into 2.5 cm/ 1 inch cubes.

2 Melt the butter or margarine in a large, heavy-based saucepan. Add the onion and garlic and fry over a low heat until soft but not coloured.

3 Add the pumpkin and toss with the onion for 2–3 minutes.

4 Add the stock and bring to the boil over a medium heat. Season to taste with salt and pepper and add the ginger, lemon juice, strips of orange rind, if using, and bay leaves or bouquet garni. Cover and simmer over a low heat for about 20 minutes, until the pumpkin is tender.

5 Discard the orange rind, if using, and the bay leaves or bouquet garni. Cool the soup slightly, then press through a strainer or process in a food processor until smooth. Pour into a clean saucepan.

6 Add the milk and reheat gently. Adjust the seasoning. Garnish with a swirl of cream, natural yogurt or fromage frais and snipped chives, and serve.

Spanish Tortilla

This classic Spanish dish is often served as part of a tapas selection.
A variety of cooked vegetables can be added to this recipe.

NUTRITIONAL INFORMATION

Calories 430	Sugars 6g
Protein 16g	Fat 20g
Carbohydrate ...50g	Saturates 4g

🥘 10 MINS   🕐 35 MINS

SERVES 4

I N G R E D I E N T S

1 kg/2 lb 4 oz waxy potatoes, thinly sliced

4 tbsp vegetable oil

1 onion, sliced

2 garlic cloves, crushed

1 green pepper, seeded and diced

2 tomatoes, seeded and chopped

25 g/1 oz canned sweetcorn, drained

6 large eggs, beaten

2 tbsp chopped parsley

salt and pepper

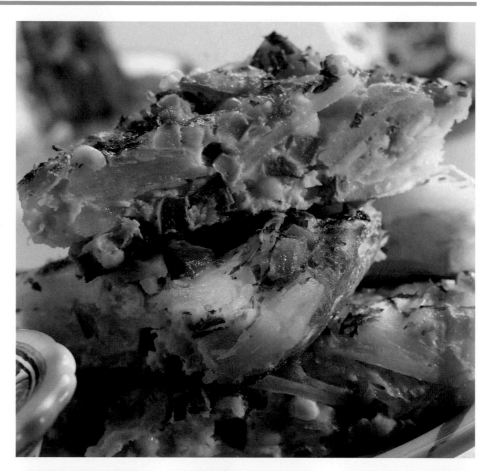

1 Parboil the potatoes in a saucepan of lightly salted boiling water for 5 minutes. Drain well.

2 Heat the oil in a large frying pan, add the potato and onions and sauté over a low heat, stirring constantly, for 5 minutes, until the potatoes have browned.

COOK'S TIP

Ensure that the handle of your pan is heatproof before placing it under the grill and be sure to use an oven glove when removing it as it will be very hot.

3 Add the garlic, diced pepper, chopped tomatoes and sweetcorn, mixing well.

4 Pour in the eggs and add the chopped parsley. Season well with salt and pepper. Cook for 10-12 minutes, until the underside is cooked through.

5 Remove the frying pan from the heat and continue to cook the tortilla under a preheated medium grill for 5-7 minutes, or until the tortilla is set and the top is golden brown.

6 Cut the tortilla into wedges or cubes, depending on your preference, and transfer to serving dishes. Serve with salad. In Spain tortillas are served hot, cold or warm.

Vegetable Medley

This is a colourful dish of shredded vegetables in a fresh garlic and honey dressing. It is delicious served with crusty bread.

NUTRITIONAL INFORMATION

Calories	209	Sugars	........10g
Protein	.........2g	Fat	..........14g
Carbohydrate	...20g	Saturates	.......2g

 15 MINS 5 MINS

SERVES 4

I N G R E D I E N T S

2 tbsp olive oil

1 potato, cut into thin strips

1 fennel bulb, cut into thin strips

2 carrots, grated

1 red onion, cut into thin strips

chopped chives and fennel fronds,
  to garnish

DRESSING

3 tbsp olive oil

1 tbsp garlic wine vinegar

1 garlic clove, crushed

1 tsp Dijon mustard

2 tsp clear honey

salt and pepper

1 Heat the olive oil in a frying pan, add the potato and fennel slices and cook over a medium heat for about 2–3 minutes, until beginning to brown. Remove from the frying pan with a slotted spoon and drain on kitchen paper.

2 Arrange the carrot, red onion, potato and fennel in separate piles on a serving platter.

3 Mix the dressing ingredients together and pour over the vegetables. Toss well and sprinkle with chopped chives and fennel fronds. Serve immediately or leave in the refrigerator until required.

VARIATION

Use mixed, grilled peppers or shredded leeks in this dish for variety, or add bean sprouts and a segmented orange, if you prefer.

Vegetable Fritters

These mixed vegetable fritters are coated in a light batter and deep-fried until golden. They are ideal with the sweet and sour dipping sauce.

NUTRITIONAL INFORMATION

Calories	479	Sugars	........18g
Protein	.........8g	Fat	..........32g
Carbohydrate	...42g	Saturates	.......5g

20 MINS   20 MINS

SERVES 4

I N G R E D I E N T S

100 g/3½ oz wholemeal flour

pinch of cayenne pepper

4 tsp olive oil

12 tbsp cold water

100 g/3½ oz broccoli florets

100 g/3½ oz cauliflower florets

50 g/1¼ oz mangetout

1 large carrot, cut into batons

1 red pepper, seeded and sliced

2 egg whites, beaten

oil, for deep-frying

salt

S A U C E

150 ml/¼ pint pineapple juice

150 ml/¼ pint vegetable stock

2 tbsp white wine vinegar

2 tbsp light brown sugar

2 tsp cornflour

2 spring onions, chopped

1 Sift the flour and a pinch of salt into a mixing bowl and add the cayenne pepper. Make a well in the centre and gradually beat in the oil and cold water to make a smooth batter.

2 Cook the vegetables in boiling water for 5 minutes and drain well.

3 Whisk the egg whites until they form peaks and gently fold them into the flour batter.

4 Dip the vegetables into the batter, turning to coat well. Drain off any excess batter. Heat the oil for deep-frying in a deep-fryer to 180°C/350°F or until a cube of bread browns in 30 seconds. Fry the coated vegetables, in batches, for 1–2 minutes, until golden. Remove from the oil with a slotted spoon and drain on kitchen paper.

5 Place all of the sauce ingredients in a pan and bring to the boil, stirring, until thickened and clear. Serve with the fritters.

Hummus & Garlic Toasts

Hummus is a real favourite spread on these flavoursome garlic toasts for a delicious starter or snack.

NUTRITIONAL INFORMATION

Calories 731	Sugars 2g
Protein 22g	Fat 55g
Carbohydrate . . .39g	Saturates 8g

 20 MINS   3 MINS

SERVES 4

I N G R E D I E N T S

HUMMUS

400 g/14 oz can chickpeas

juice of 1 large lemon

6 tbsp tahini (sesame seed paste)

2 tbsp olive oil

2 garlic cloves, crushed

salt and pepper

chopped coriander and black olives, to garnish

TOASTS

1 ciabatta loaf, sliced

2 garlic cloves, crushed

1 tbsp chopped coriander

4 tbsp olive oil

COOK'S TIP

Make the hummus 1 day in advance, and chill, covered, in the refrigerator until required. Garnish and serve.

1 To make the hummus, firstly drain the chickpeas, reserving a little of the liquid. Put the chickpeas and liquid in a food processor and process, gradually adding the reserved liquid and lemon juice. Blend well after each addition until smooth.

2 Stir in the tahini (sesame seed paste) and all but 1 teaspoon of the olive oil. Add the garlic, season to taste and blend again until smooth.

3 Spoon the hummus into a serving dish and smooth the top. Drizzle the remaining olive oil over the top, garnish with chopped coriander and olives. Set aside in the refrigerator to chill while you are preparing the toasts.

4 Place the slices of ciabatta on a grill rack in a single layer.

5 Mix the garlic, coriander and olive oil together and drizzle over the bread slices. Cook under a hot grill, turning once, for about 2–3 minutes, until golden brown. Serve the toasts immediately with the hummus.

Garlicky Mushroom Pakoras

Whole mushrooms are dunked in a spiced garlicky batter and deep-fried until golden. They are at their most delicious served piping hot.

NUTRITIONAL INFORMATION

Calories	297	Sugars	........3g
Protein	.........5g	Fat	.........21g
Carbohydrate	...24g	Saturates	.......2g

🍲 20 MINS   🕐 10–15 MINS

SERVES 6

INGREDIENTS

175 g/6 oz gram flour

½ tsp salt

¼ tsp baking powder

1 tsp cumin seeds

½–1 tsp chilli powder

200 ml/7 fl oz water

2 garlic cloves, crushed

1 small onion, finely chopped

vegetable oil, for deep-frying

500 g/1 lb 2 oz button mushrooms, trimmed and wiped

lemon wedges and coriander sprigs, to garnish

1 Put the gram flour, salt, baking powder, cumin and chilli powder into a bowl and mix well together. Make a well in the centre of the mixture and gradually stir in the water, mixing thoroughly to form a batter.

2 Stir the crushed garlic and the chopped onion into the batter and leave the mixture to infuse for 10 minutes. One-third fill a deep-fat fryer or pan with vegetable oil and heat to 180°C/350°F or until a cube of bread browns in 30 seconds. Lower the basket into the hot oil.

3 Meanwhile, mix the mushrooms into the batter, stirring to coat. Remove a few at a time and place them into the hot oil. Fry for about 2 minutes, or until golden brown.

4 Remove the mushrooms from the pan with a slotted spoon and drain on kitchen paper while you are cooking the remainder in the same way.

5 Serve hot, sprinkled with coarse salt and garnished with lemon wedges and coriander sprigs.

COOK'S TIP

Gram flour, also known as besan flour, is a pale yellow flour made from chickpeas. It is now readily available from larger supermarkets, as well as Indian food shops and some ethnic delicatessens. Gram flour is also used to make onion bhajis.

Onions à la Grecque

This is a well-known method of cooking vegetables and is perfect with shallots or onions, served with a crisp salad.

NUTRITIONAL INFORMATION

Calories ....200 Sugars 26g
Protein ....2g Fat 9g
Carbohydrate ...28g Saturates 1g

10 MINS   15 MINS

SERVES 4

INGREDIENTS

450 g/1 lb shallots

3 tbsp olive oil

3 tbsp clear honey

2 tbsp garlic wine vinegar

3 tbsp dry white wine

1 tbsp tomato purée

2 celery stalks, sliced

2 tomatoes, seeded and chopped

salt and pepper

chopped celery leaves, to garnish

1 Peel the shallots. Heat the oil in a large saucepan, add the shallots and cook, stirring, for 3–5 minutes, or until they begin to brown.

2 Add the honey and cook over a high heat for a further 30 seconds, then add the garlic wine vinegar and dry white wine, stirring well.

3 Stir in the tomato purée, celery and tomatoes and bring the mixture to the boil. Cook over a high heat for 5–6 minutes. Season to taste and leave to cool slightly.

4 Garnish with chopped celery leaves and serve warm. Alternatively chill in the refrigerator before serving.

Mixed Bean Pâté

This is a really quick starter to prepare if canned beans are used. Choose a wide variety of beans for colour and flavour.

NUTRITIONAL INFORMATION

Calories	126	Sugars	.........3g
Protein	.........5g	Fat	..........6g
Carbohydrate	...13g	Saturates	.......1g

 45 MINS 0 MINS

SERVES 4

INGREDIENTS

400 g/14 oz can mixed beans, drained

2 tbsp olive oil

juice of 1 lemon

2 garlic cloves, crushed

1 tbsp chopped coriander

2 spring onions, chopped

salt and pepper

shredded spring onions, to garnish

1 Rinse the beans thoroughly under cold running water and drain well.

2 Transfer the beans to a food processor or blender and process until smooth. Alternatively, place the beans in a bowl and mash thoroughly with a fork or potato masher.

3 Add the olive oil, lemon juice, garlic, coriander and spring onions and blend until fairly smooth. Season with salt and pepper to taste.

4 Transfer the pâté to a serving bowl and chill in the refrigerator for at least 30 minutes.

5 Garnish with shredded spring onions and serve.

Mixed Bhajis

These small bhajis are often served as accompaniments to a main meal, but they are delicious as a starter with a small salad and yogurt sauce.

NUTRITIONAL INFORMATION

Calories 414	Sugars 7g
Protein 9g	Fat 26g
Carbohydrate . . .38g	Saturates 3g

  25 MINS   30 MINS

SERVES 4

INGREDIENTS

BHAJIS

175 g/6 oz gram flour

1 tsp bicarbonate of soda

2 tsp ground coriander

1 tsp garam masala

1½ tsp turmeric

1½ tsp chilli powder

2 tbsp chopped coriander

1 small onion, halved and sliced

1 small leek, sliced

100 g/3½ oz cooked cauliflower

9–12 tbsp cold water

salt and pepper

vegetable oil, for deep-frying

SAUCE

150 ml/¼ pint natural yogurt

2 tbsp chopped mint

½ tsp turmeric

1 garlic clove, crushed

mint sprigs, to garnish

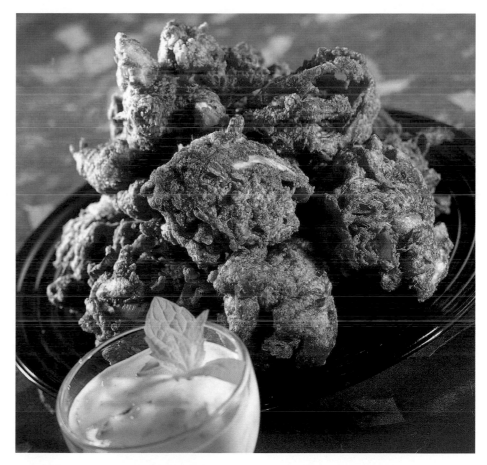

1 Sift the flour, bicarbonate of soda and salt to taste into a mixing bowl and add the spices and fresh coriander. Mix thoroughly.

2 Divide the mixture into 3 and place in separate bowls. Stir the onion into one bowl, the leek into another and the cauliflower into the third bowl. Add 3–4 tbsp of water to each bowl and mix each to form a smooth paste.

3 Heat the oil for deep-frying in a deep fryer to 180°C/350°F or until a cube of bread browns in 30 seconds. Using 2 dessert spoons, form the mixture into rounds and cook each in the oil for 3–4 minutes, until browned. Remove with a slotted spoon and drain well on absorbent kitchen paper. Keep the bhajis warm in the oven while cooking the remainder.

4 Mix all of the sauce ingredients together and pour into a small serving bowl. Garnish with mint sprigs and serve with the warm bhajis.

Garlic Mushrooms on Toast

This is so simple to prepare and looks great if you use a variety of mushrooms for shape and texture.

NUTRITIONAL INFORMATION

Calories	366	Sugars 2g
Protein	.........9g	Fat 18g
Carbohydrate	...45g	Saturates 4g

 10 MINS 10 MINS

SERVES 4

I N G R E D I E N T S

75 g/2¾ oz margarine

2 garlic cloves, crushed

350 g/12 oz mixed mushrooms, such as open-cap, button, oyster and shiitake, sliced

8 slices French bread

1 tbsp chopped parsley

salt and pepper

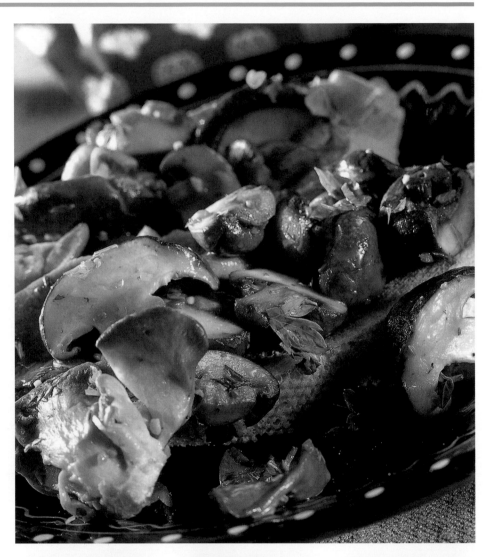

1 Melt the margarine in a frying pan. Add the crushed garlic and cook, stirring constantly, for 30 seconds.

2 Add the mushrooms and cook, turning occasionally, for 5 minutes.

3 Toast the French bread slices under a preheated medium grill for 2–3 minutes, turning once. Transfer the toasts to a serving plate.

COOK'S TIP

Always store mushrooms for a maximum of 24–36 hours in the refrigerator, in paper bags, as they sweat in plastic. Wild mushrooms should be washed but other varieties can simply be wiped with kitchen paper.

4 Toss the parsley into the mushrooms, mixing well, and season well with salt and pepper to taste.

5 Spoon the mushroom mixture over the bread and serve immediately.

Corn & Potato Fritters

An ideal supper dish for two, or for one if you halve the quantities.
You can use the remaining corn in another recipe.

NUTRITIONAL INFORMATION

Calories	639	Sugars	........17g
Protein	........28g	Fat	..........31g
Carbohydrate	...65g	Saturates	.......9g

🥔 20 MINS   🕐 20 MINS

SERVES 2

INGREDIENTS

2 tbsp oil

1 small onion, thinly sliced

1 garlic clove, crushed

350 g/12 oz potatoes

200 g/7 oz can of sweetcorn, drained

½ tsp dried oregano

1 egg, beaten

60 g/2 oz grated Edam or Gouda cheese

salt and pepper

2–4 eggs

2–4 tomatoes, sliced

parsley sprigs, to garnish

1 Heat 1 tablespoon of the oil in a non-stick frying pan. Add the onion and garlic and fry very gently, stirring frequently, until soft, but only lightly coloured. Remove from the heat.

2 Grate the potatoes coarsely into a bowl and mix in the sweetcorn, oregano, beaten egg and salt and pepper to taste. Add the fried onion.

3 Heat the remaining oil in the frying pan. Divide the potato mixture in half

and add to the pan to make 2 oval-shaped cakes, levelling and shaping the cakes with a palette knife.

4 Cook the fritters over a low heat for about 10 minutes, until golden brown underneath and almost cooked through, keeping them tidily in shape with the palette knife and loosening so they don't stick.

5 Sprinkle each potato fritter with the grated cheese and place under a preheated moderately hot grill until golden brown.

6 Meanwhile, poach 1 or 2 eggs for each person until just cooked. Transfer the fritters to warmed plates and top with the eggs and sliced tomatoes. Garnish with parsley and serve at once.

Mixed Bean Pan-Fry

Fresh green beans have a wonderful flavour that is hard to beat.
If you cannot find fresh beans, use thawed, frozen beans instead.

NUTRITIONAL INFORMATION

Calories	179	Sugars	.........4g
Protein	........10g	Fat	...........11g
Carbohydrate	...10g	Saturates	.......1g

 10 MINS   15 MINS

SERVES 4

I N G R E D I E N T S

350 g/12 oz mixed green beans, such as French and broad beans, podded

2 tbsp vegetable oil

2 garlic cloves, crushed

1 red onion, halved and sliced

225 g/8 oz firm marinated tofu, diced

1 tbsp lemon juice

½ tsp turmeric

1 tsp ground mixed spice

150 ml/¼ pint vegetable stock

2 tsp sesame seeds

1 Trim and chop the French beans and set aside until required.

2 Heat the oil in a medium frying pan. Add the garlic and onion and sauté, stirring frequently, over a low heat for 2 minutes.

3 Add the tofu and cook for 2–3 minutes, until just beginning to turn golden brown.

4 Add the French beans and broad beans. Stir in the lemon juice, turmeric, ground mixed spice and vegetable stock and bring to the boil over a medium heat.

5 Reduce the heat and simmer for 5–7 minutes, or until the beans are tender. Sprinkle with sesame seeds and serve immediately.

VARIATION
Use smoked tofu instead of marinated tofu for an alternative and quite distinctive flavour.

Scrambled Tofu

This is a delicious dish which would serve equally well as a light lunch or supper and makes an excellent after-school snack.

NUTRITIONAL INFORMATION

Calories . . . . . . .392 Sugars 6g

Protein . . . . .16g Fat 22g

Carbohydrate . . .35g Saturates 4g

 5-10 MINS   5 MINS

SERVES 4

I N G R E D I E N T S

75 g/2¾ oz margarine

450 g/1 lb marinated, firm tofu

1 red onion, chopped

1 red pepper, seeded and chopped

4 ciabatta rolls

2 tbsp chopped mixed herbs

salt and pepper

fresh herbs, to garnish

1 Melt the margarine in a frying pan and crumble the tofu into it.

2 Add the onion and pepper and cook, stirring occasionally, for 3–4 minutes.

COOK'S TIP

Marinated tofu adds extra flavour to this dish. Smoked tofu could be used instead. Rub the cut surface of a garlic clove over the toasted ciabatta rolls for extra flavour.

3 Meanwhile, slice the ciabatta rolls in half and toast them under a hot grill for about 2–3 minutes, turning once.

4 Remove the toasts and transfer to a serving plate.

5 Add the mixed herbs to the tofu mixture, combine and season to taste with salt and pepper.

6 Spoon the tofu mixture on to the toast and garnish with fresh herbs. Serve at once.

Refried Beans with Tortillas

Refried beans are a classic Mexican dish and are usually served as an accompaniment. They are, however, delicious served with warm tortillas.

NUTRITIONAL INFORMATION

Calories 519   Sugars 14g
Protein . . . . .25g   Fat 28g
Carbohydrate . . .44g   Saturates 9g

 15 MINS   15 MINS

SERVES 4

I N G R E D I E N T S

B E A N S

2 tbsp olive oil

1 onion, finely chopped

3 garlic cloves, crushed

1 green chilli, chopped

400 g/14 oz can red kidney beans, drained

400 g/14 oz can pinto beans, drained

2 tbsp chopped coriander

150 ml/¼ pint vegetable stock

8 wheat tortillas

25 g/1 oz grated Cheddar cheese

salt and pepper

R E L I S H

4 spring onions, chopped

1 red onion, chopped

1 green chilli, chopped

1 tbsp garlic wine vinegar

1 tsp caster sugar

1 tomato, chopped

1 Heat the oil for the beans in a large frying pan over a medium heat. Add the onion and sauté, stirring frequently, for 3–5 minutes. Add the garlic and chilli and cook for 1 minute.

2 Mash the beans with a potato masher and stir into the pan, together with the coriander.

3 Stir in the vegetable stock and cook the beans, stirring constantly, for 5 minutes until soft and pulpy.

4 Meanwhile, place the tortillas on a baking tray and heat through in a preheated oven, 180°C/350°F/Gas Mark 4, oven for about 1–2 minutes.

5 Mix the relish ingredients together. Spoon the beans into a serving dish and top with the cheese. Season to taste with salt and pepper. Roll the warm tortillas and serve with the onion relish and refried beans.

Buck Rarebit

This substantial version of cheese on toast – a creamy cheese sauce topped with a poached egg – makes a tasty, filling snack.

NUTRITIONAL INFORMATION

Calories 478	Sugars 2g
Protein 29g	Fat 34g
Carbohydrate ...14g	Saturates 20g

 10 MINS   15-20 MINS

SERVES 4

INGREDIENTS

350 g/12 oz mature Cheddar

125 g/4½ oz Gouda, Gruyère or Emmental cheese

1 tsp mustard powder

1 tsp wholegrain mustard

2-4 tbsp brown ale, cider or milk

½ tsp vegetarian Worcestershire sauce

4 thick slices white or brown bread

4 eggs

salt and pepper

TO GARNISH

tomato wedges

watercress sprigs

VARIATION

For a change, you can use part or all Stilton or other blue cheese; the appearance is not so attractive but the flavour is very good.

1 Grate the cheeses and place in a non-stick saucepan.

2 Add the mustards, seasoning, brown ale, cider or milk and vegetarian Worcestershire sauce and mix well.

3 Heat the cheese mixture gently, stirring until it has melted and is completely thick and creamy. Remove from the heat and leave to cool a little.

4 Toast the slices of bread on each side under a preheated grill then spread the rarebit mixture evenly over each piece. Put under a moderate grill until golden brown and bubbling.

5 Meanwhile, poach the eggs. If using a poacher, grease the cups, heat the water in the pan and, when just boiling, break the eggs into the cups. Cover and simmer for 4-5 minutes until just set. Alternatively, bring about 4 cm/1½ inches of water to the boil in a frying pan or large saucepan and for each egg quickly swirl the water with a knife and drop the egg into the "hole" created. Cook for about 4 minutes until just set.

6 Top the rarebits with a poached egg and serve garnished with tomato wedges and sprigs of watercress.

Vegetable Kebabs

These kebabs, made from a spicy vegetable mixture, are delightfully easy to make and taste delicious.

NUTRITIONAL INFORMATION

Calories 268   Sugars 1g
Protein . . . . .2g   Fat 25g
Carbohydrate . . . .9g   Saturates 3g

20 MINS   25-30 MINS

MAKES 12

I N G R E D I E N T S

2 large potatoes, sliced

1 medium onion, sliced

½ medium cauliflower, cut into small florets

50 g/1¾ oz peas

1 tbsp spinach purée

2-3 green chillies

fresh coriander leaves

1 tsp finely chopped root ginger

1 tsp crushed garlic

1 tsp ground coriander

1 pinch turmeric

1 tsp salt

60 g/1¾ oz breadcrumbs

300 ml/½ pint vegetable oil

fresh chilli strips, to garnish

1 Place the potatoes, onion and cauliflower florets in a pan of water and bring to the boil. Reduce the heat and simmer until the potatoes are cooked through. Remove the vegetables from the pan with a slotted spoon and drain thoroughly. Set aside.

2 Add the peas and spinach to the vegetables and mix, mashing down thoroughly with a fork.

3 Using a sharp knife, finely chop the green chillies and fresh coriander leaves.

4 Mix the chillies and coriander with the ginger, garlic, ground coriander, turmeric and salt.

5 Blend the spice mixture into the vegetables, mixing with a fork to make a paste.

6 Scatter the breadcrumbs on to a large plate.

7 Break off 10-12 small balls from the spice paste. Flatten them with the palm of your hand to make flat, round shapes.

8 Dip each kebab in the breadcrumbs, coating well.

9 Heat the oil in a heavy-based frying-pan and shallow-fry the kabobs, in batches, until golden brown, turning occasionally. Transfer to serving plates and garnish with fresh chilli strips. Serve hot.

Vegetable Hash

This is a quick one-pan dish which is ideal for a snack. Packed with colour and flavour it is very versatile, as you can add other vegetables.

NUTRITIONAL INFORMATION

Calories 182   Sugars 6g
Protein ....5g   Fat 4g
Carbohydrate ...34g   Saturates 0.5g

 15 MINS   30 MINS

SERVES 4

I N G R E D I E N T S

675 g/1½ lb potatoes, cubed

1 tbsp olive oil

2 garlic cloves, crushed

1 green pepper, seeded and cubed

1 yellow pepper, seeded and cubed

3 tomatoes, diced

75 g/2¾ oz button mushrooms, halved

1 tbsp vegetarian Worcestershire sauce

2 tbsp chopped basil

salt and pepper

basil sprigs, to garnish

warm, crusty bread, to serve

1 Cook the potatoes in a saucepan of boiling salted water for 7–8 minutes. Drain well and reserve.

2 Heat the olive oil in a large, heavy-based frying pan. Add the potatoes and cook, stirring constantly, for 8–10 minutes, until browned.

3 Add the garlic and peppers and cook, stirring frequently, for 2–3 minutes.

4 Stir in the tomatoes and mushrooms and cook, stirring frequently, for 5–6 minutes.

5 Stir in the vegetarian Worcestershire sauce and basil and season to taste with salt and pepper. Transfer to a warm serving dish, garnish with basil sprigs and serve with warm crusty bread.

COOK'S TIP

Most brands of Worcestershire sauce contain anchovies, so check the label to make sure you choose a vegetarian variety.

Falafel

These are a very tasty, well-known Middle Eastern dish of small chickpea based balls, spiced and deep-fried.

NUTRITIONAL INFORMATION

Calories 491	Sugars 3g	
Protein 15g	Fat 30g	
Carbohydrate . . .43g	Saturates 3g	

   25 MINS   🕑 10–15 MINS

SERVES 4

I N G R E D I E N T S

675 g/1½ lb canned chickpeas, drained

1 red onion, chopped

3 garlic cloves, crushed

100 g/3½ oz wholemeal bread

2 small fresh red chillies

1 tsp ground cumin

1 tsp ground coriander

½ tsp turmeric

1 tbsp chopped coriander,
    plus extra to garnish

1 egg, beaten

100 g/3½ oz wholemeal breadcrumbs

vegetable oil, for deep-frying

salt and pepper

tomato and cucumber salad and lemon
    wedges, to serve

1 Put the chickpeas, onion, garlic, bread, chillies, spices and coriander in a food processor and process for 30 seconds. Stir and season to taste with salt and pepper.

2 Remove the mixture from the food processor and shape into walnut-sized balls.

3 Place the beaten egg in a shallow bowl and place the wholemeal breadcrumbs on a plate. Dip the balls first into the egg to coat and then roll them in the breadcrumbs, shaking off any excess.

4 Heat the oil for deep-frying to 180°C/350°F or until a cube of bread browns in 30 seconds. Fry the falafel, in batches if necessary, for 2–3 minutes, until crisp and browned. Remove from the oil with a slotted spoon and dry on absorbent kitchen paper. Garnish with coriander and serve with a tomato and cucumber salad and lemon wedges.

Chow Mein

Egg noodles are cooked and then fried with a colourful variety
of vegetables to make this well-known and ever-popular dish.

NUTRITIONAL INFORMATION

Calories 669   Sugars 9g
Protein ....19g   Fat 23g
Carbohydrate ..100g   Saturates 4g

15 MINS   10 MINS

SERVES 4

I N G R E D I E N T S

500 g/1 lb 2 oz egg noodles

4 tbsp vegetable oil

1 onion, thinly sliced

2 carrots, cut into thin sticks

125 g/4½ oz button mushrooms, quartered

125 g/4½ oz mangetout

½ cucumber, cut into sticks

125 g/4½ oz spinach, shredded

125 g/4½ oz beansprouts

2 tbsp dark soy sauce

1 tbsp sherry

1 tsp salt

1 tsp sugar

1 tsp cornflour

1 tsp sesame oil

COOK'S TIP

For a spicy hot chow mein,
add 1 tablespoon chilli sauce
or substitute chilli oil for the
sesame oil.

1 Cook the noodles according to the instructions on the packet. Drain and rinse under cold running water until cool. Set aside.

2 Heat 3 tablespoons of the vegetable oil in a preheated wok or frying pan. Add the onion and carrots, and stir-fry for 1 minute. Add the mushrooms, mangetout and cucumber and stir-fry for 1 minute.

3 Stir in the remaining vegetable oil and add the drained noodles, together with the spinach and beansprouts.

4 Blend together all the remaining ingredients and pour over the noodles and vegetables.

5 Stir-fry until the noodle mixture is thoroughly heated through, transfer to a warm serving dish and serve.

Spicy Japanese Noodles

These noodles are highly spiced with chilli and flavoured with sesame seeds for a nutty taste that is a true delight.

NUTRITIONAL INFORMATION

Calories 381	Sugars 12g
Protein 11g	Fat 13g
Carbohydrate . . .59g	Saturates 2g

 5 MINS   15 MINS

SERVES 4

INGREDIENTS

500 g/1 lb 2 oz fresh Japanese noodles

1 tbsp sesame oil

1 tbsp sesame seeds

1 tbsp sunflower oil

1 red onion, sliced

100 g/3½ oz mangetout,

175 g/6 oz carrots, thinly sliced

350 g/12 oz white cabbage, shredded

3 tbsp sweet chilli sauce

2 spring onions, sliced, to garnish

1 Bring a large saucepan of water to the boil. Add the Japanese noodles to the pan and cook for 2–3 minutes. Drain the noodles thoroughly.

2 Toss the noodles with the sesame oil and sesame seeds.

3 Heat the sunflower oil in a large preheated wok.

4 Add the onion slices, mangetout, carrot slices and shredded cabbage to the wok and stir-fry for about 5 minutes.

5 Add the sweet chilli sauce to the wok and cook, stirring occasionally, for a further 2 minutes.

6 Add the sesame noodles to the wok, toss thoroughly to combine and heat through for a further 2–3 minutes. (You may wish to serve the noodles separately, so transfer them to the serving bowls.)

7 Transfer the Japanese noodles and spicy vegetables to warm individual serving bowls, scatter over the sliced spring onions to garnish and serve immediately.

COOK'S TIP

If fresh Japanese noodles are difficult to get hold of, use dried rice noodles or thin egg noodles instead.

Risotto Verde

Risotto is an Italian dish which is easy to make and uses arborio rice, onion and garlic as a base for a range of savoury recipes.

NUTRITIONAL INFORMATION

Calories 374	Sugars 5g
Protein 10g	Fat 9g
Carbohydrate ...55g	Saturates 2g

5 MINS   35 MINS

SERVES 4

INGREDIENTS

1.75 litres/3 pints vegetable stock

2 tbsp olive oil

2 garlic cloves, crushed

2 leeks, shredded

225 g/8 oz arborio rice

300 ml/½ pint dry white wine

4 tbsp chopped mixed herbs

225 g/8 oz baby spinach

3 tbsp natural yogurt

salt and pepper

shredded leek, to garnish

1 Pour the stock into a large saucepan and bring to the boil. Reduce the heat to a simmer.

2 Meanwhile, heat the oil in a separate pan. Add the garlic and leeks and sauté over a low heat, stirring occasionally, for 2–3 minutes, until softened.

3 Stir in the rice and cook for 2 minutes, stirring until each grain is coated with oil.

4 Pour in half of the wine and a little of the hot stock. Cook over a low heat until all of the liquid has been absorbed. Add the remaining stock and the wine, a little at a time, and cook over a low heat for 25 minutes, or until the rice is creamy.

5 Stir in the chopped mixed herbs and baby spinach, season to taste with salt and pepper and cook for 2 minutes.

6 Stir in the natural yogurt. Transfer to a warm serving dish, garnish with the shredded leek and serve immediately.

COOK'S TIP

Do not try to hurry the process of cooking the risotto as the rice must absorb the liquid slowly in order for it to reach the correct consistency.

Special Fried Rice

In this simple recipe, cooked rice is fried with vegetables and cashew nuts. It can either be eaten on its own or served as an accompaniment.

NUTRITIONAL INFORMATION

Calories 355	Sugars 6g
Protein 9g	Fat 15g
Carbohydrate ...48g	Saturates 3g

  10 MINS   30 MINS

SERVES 4

I N G R E D I E N T S

175 g/6 oz long grain rice

60 g/2 oz cashew nuts

1 carrot

½ cucumber

1 yellow pepper

2 spring onions

2 tbsp vegetable oil

1 garlic clove, crushed

125 g/4½ oz frozen peas, thawed

1 tbsp soy sauce

1 tsp salt

coriander leaves, to garnish

1 Bring a large pan of water to the boil. Add the rice and simmer for 15 minutes. Tip the rice into a strainer and rinse; drain thoroughly.

COOK'S TIP

You can replace any of the vegetables in this recipe with others suitable for a stir-fry, and using leftover rice makes this a perfect last-minute dish.

2 Heat a wok or large, heavy-based frying pan, add the cashew nuts and dry-fry until lightly browned. Remove and set aside.

3 Cut the carrot in half along the length, then slice thinly into semi-circles. Halve the cucumber and remove the seeds, using a teaspoon, then dice the flesh. Seed and slice the pepper and chop the spring onions.

4 Heat the oil in a wok or large frying pan. Add the prepared vegetables and the garlic. Stir-fry for 3 minutes. Add the rice, peas, soy sauce and salt. Continue to stir-fry until well mixed and thoroughly heated.

5 Stir in the reserved cashew nuts. Transfer to a warmed serving dish, garnish with coriander leaves and serve immediately.

Kitchouri

The traditional breakfast plate of kedgeree reputedly has its roots in this Indian flavoured rice dish, which English colonists adopted.

NUTRITIONAL INFORMATION

Calories 318	Sugars 5g
Protein 12g	Fat 10g
Carbohydrate . . .48g	Saturates 6g

🍲 10 MINS   🕐 30 MINS

SERVES 4

I N G R E D I E N T S

2 tbsp vegetable ghee or butter

I red onion, finely chopped

1 garlic clove, crushed

½ celery stick, finely chopped

1 tsp turmeric

½ tsp garam masala

1 green chilli, seeded and finely chopped

½ tsp cumin seeds

1 tbsp chopped coriander

125 g/4½ oz basmati rice,
   rinsed under cold water

125 g/4½ oz green lentils

300 ml/½ pint vegetable juice

600 ml/1 pint vegetable stock

1 Heat the ghee or butter in a large heavy-based saucepan. Add the onion, garlic and celery and cook for about 5 minutes, until soft.

2 Add the turmeric, garam masala, green chilli, cumin seeds and coriander. Cook over a moderate heat, stirring constantly, for about 1 minute, until fragrant.

3 Add the rice and lentils and cook for 1 minute, until the rice is translucent.

4 Pour the vegetable juice and stock into the saucepan and bring to the boil over a medium heat. Cover and simmer over a low heat, stirring occasionally, for about 20 minutes, or until the lentils are cooked. (They should be tender when pressed between two fingers.)

5 Transfer the kitchouri to a warmed serving dish and serve piping hot.

COOK'S TIP

This is a versatile dish, and can be served as a great-tasting and satisfying one-pot meal. It can also be served as a winter lunch dish with tomatoes and yogurt.

Thai Jasmine Rice

Every Thai meal has as its centrepiece a big bowl of steaming, fluffy Thai jasmine rice, to which salt should not be added.

NUTRITIONAL INFORMATION

Calories 239	Sugars 0g	
Protein 5g	Fat 2g	
Carbohydrate ...54g	Saturates 0.6g	

 5 MINS   10–15 MINS

SERVES 4

INGREDIENTS

OPEN PAN METHOD

225 g/8 oz Thai jasmine rice

1 litre/1¾ pints water

ABSORPTION METHOD

225 g/8 oz Thai jasmine rice

450 ml/16 fl oz water

COOK'S TIP

Thai jasmine rice can be frozen. Freeze in a plastic sealed container. Frozen rice is ideal for stir-fry dishes, as the process seems to separate the grains.

1 For the open pan method, rinse the rice in a strainer under cold running water and leave to drain.

2 Bring the water to the boil. Add the rice, stir once and return to a medium boil. Cook, uncovered, for 8–10 minutes, until tender.

3 Drain thoroughly and fork through lightly before serving.

4 For the absorption method, rinse the rice under cold running water.

5 Put the rice and water into a saucepan and bring to the boil. Stir once and then cover the pan tightly. Lower the heat as much as possible. Cook for 10 minutes. Leave to rest for 5 minutes.

6 Fork through lightly and serve the rice immediately.

White Lentils

This dhal is dry when cooked, so give it a baghaar dressing. It makes an excellent accompaniment to any meal of kormas.

NUTRITIONAL INFORMATION

Calories 129   Sugars 1g
Protein ....6g   Fat 6g
Carbohydrate ...14g   Saturates 1g

5 MINS   45 MINS

SERVES 4

INGREDIENTS

100 g/3½ oz urid dhal

1 tsp finely chopped root ginger

600 ml/1 pint water

1 tsp salt

1 tsp pepper

2 tbsp vegetable ghee

2 garlic cloves

2 fresh red chillies, finely chopped

mint leaves, to garnish

chapatis, to serve

1 Rinse the lentils thoroughly and put them in a large saucepan, together with the ginger.

2 Add the water and bring to a boil. Cover and simmer over a medium heat for about 30 minutes. Check to see whether the lentils are cooked by rubbing them between your finger and thumb. If they are still a little hard in the middle, cook for a further 5–7 minutes. If necessary, remove the lid and cook until any remaining water has evaporated.

3 Add the salt and pepper to the lentils, mix well and set aside.

4 To make the baghaar, heat the ghee in a separate saucepan. Add the cloves of garlic and chopped red chillies and stir well to mix thoroughly.

5 Pour the garlic and chilli mixture over the lentils and then garnish with the fresh mint leaves.

6 Transfer the white lentils to warm individual serving dishes and serve hot with chapatis .

COOK'S TIP

Ghee was traditionally made from clarified butter, which can withstand higher temperatures than ordinary butter. Vegetable ghee has largely replaced it now because it is lower in saturated fats.

Deep South Rice & Beans

Cajun spices add a flavour of the American Deep South to this colourful rice and red kidney bean salad.

NUTRITIONAL INFORMATION

Calories 336	Sugars 8g	
Protein 7g	Fat 13g	
Carbohydrate ...51g	Saturates 2g	

 10 MINS   15 MINS

SERVES 4

I N G R E D I E N T S

175 g/6 oz long grain rice

4 tbsp olive oil

1 small green pepper, seeded and chopped

1 small red pepper, seeded and chopped

1 onion, finely chopped

1 small red or green chilli, seeded and finely chopped

2 tomatoes, chopped

125 g/4½ oz canned red kidney beans, rinsed and drained

1 tbsp chopped fresh basil

2 tsp chopped fresh thyme

1 tsp Cajun spice

salt and pepper

fresh basil leaves, to garnish

1 Cook the rice in plenty of boiling, lightly salted water for about 12 minutes, until just tender. Rinse with cold water and drain well.

2 Meanwhile, heat the olive oil in a frying pan and fry the green and red peppers and onion gently for about 5 minutes, until softened.

3 Add the chilli and tomatoes, and cook for a further 2 minutes.

4 Add the vegetable mixture and red kidney beans to the rice. Stir well to combine thoroughly.

5 Stir the chopped herbs and Cajun spice into the rice mixture. Season to taste with salt and pepper, and serve, garnished with basil leaves.

Onion Dhal

This dhal is semi-dry when cooked, so it is best to serve it with a dish which has a sauce. Ordinary onions can be used as a substitute.

NUTRITIONAL INFORMATION

Calories 232   Sugars 1g
Protein ....6g   Fat 17g
Carbohydrate ...15g   Saturates 2g

5 MINS   30 MINS

SERVES 4

INGREDIENTS

100 g/3½ oz masoor dhal

6 tbsp vegetable oil

1 small bunch spring onions, chopped

1 tsp finely chopped root ginger

1 tsp crushed garlic

½ tsp chilli powder

½ tsp turmeric

300 ml/½ pint water

1 tsp salt

1 fresh green chilli, finely chopped

fresh coriander leaves

1 Rinse the lentils thoroughly and set aside until required.

2 Heat the oil in a heavy-based saucepan. Add the spring onions to the pan and fry over a medium heat, stirring frequently, until lightly browned.

3 Reduce the heat and add the ginger, garlic, chilli powder and turmeric. Briefly stir-fry the spring onions with the spices. Add the lentils and mix to blend together.

4 Add the water to the lentil mixture, reduce the heat to low and cook for 20–25 minutes.

5 When the lentils are cooked thoroughly, add the salt and stir gently to mix well.

6 Transfer the onion lentils to a serving dish. Garnish with the chopped green chillies and fresh coriander leaves and serve immediately.

COOK'S TIP

Masoor dhal are small, round, pale orange split lentils. They turn a pale yellow colour when cooked.

Creamy Vegetable Curry

Vegetables are cooked in a mildly spiced curry sauce with yogurt and fresh coriander stirred in just before serving.

NUTRITIONAL INFORMATION

Calories 423   Sugars 24g
Protein . . . . .16g   Fat 19g
Carbohydrate . . .50g   Saturates 7g

 20 MINS   25 MINS

SERVES 4

INGREDIENTS

2 tbsp sunflower oil

1 onion, sliced

2 tsp cumin seeds

2 tbsp ground coriander

1 tsp ground turmeric

2 tsp ground ginger

1 tsp chopped fresh red chilli

2 garlic cloves, chopped

400 g/14 oz can chopped tomatoes

3 tbsp powdered coconut mixed with
   300 ml/½ pint boiling water

1 small cauliflower, broken into florets

2 courgettes, sliced

2 carrots, sliced

1 potato, diced

400 g/14 oz can chickpeas,
   drained and rinsed

150 ml/¼ pint thick natural yogurt

2 tbsp mango chutney

3 tbsp chopped fresh coriander

salt and pepper

fresh herbs, to garnish

1 Heat the oil in a saucepan and fry the onion until softened. Add the cumin, ground coriander, turmeric, ginger, chilli and garlic and fry for 1 minute.

2 Add the tomatoes and coconut mixture and mix well.

3 Add the cauliflower florets, courgettes, carrots, diced potato and chickpeas and season to taste with salt and pepper. Cover and simmer for 20 minutes, until the vegetables are tender.

4 Stir in the yogurt, mango chutney and fresh coriander and heat through gently, but do not boil. Transfer to a warm serving dish, garnish with fresh herbs and serve.

Red Curry with Cashews

This is a wonderfully quick dish to prepare. If you don't have time to prepare the curry paste, it can be bought ready-made.

NUTRITIONAL INFORMATION

Calories 274   Sugars 5g
Protein ....10g   Fat 10g
Carbohydrate ...38g   Saturates 3g

 25 MINS   🕐 15 MINS

SERVES 4

I N G R E D I E N T S

250 ml/9 fl oz coconut milk

1 kaffir lime leaf

¼ tsp light soy sauce

60 g/2 oz/4 baby corn cobs, halved lengthways

125 g/4½ oz broccoli florets

125 g/4½ oz French beans, cut into 5 cm/2 inch pieces

25 g/1 oz cashew nuts

15 fresh basil leaves

1 tbsp chopped coriander

1 tbsp chopped roast peanuts, to garnish

R E D   C U R R Y   P A S T E

7 fresh red chillies, halved, seeded and blanched

2 tsp cumin seeds

2 tsp coriander seeds

2.5 cm/1 inch piece galangal, chopped

½ stalk lemon grass, chopped

1 tsp salt

grated rind of 1 lime

4 garlic cloves, chopped

3 shallots, chopped

2 kaffir lime leaves, shredded

1 tbsp vegetable oil

---

1 To make the curry paste, grind all the ingredients together in a large mortar with a pestle or a grinder. Alternatively, process briefly in a food processor. The quantity of red curry paste is more than required for this recipe. However, it will keep for up to 3 weeks in a sealed container in the refrigerator.

2 Put a wok or large, heavy-based frying pan over a high heat, add 3 tablespoons of the red curry paste and stir until it gives off its aroma. Reduce the heat to medium.

3 Add the coconut milk, kaffir lime leaf, light soy sauce, baby corn cobs, broccoli florets, French beans and cashew nuts. Bring to the boil and simmer for about 10 minutes, until the vegetables are cooked, but still firm and crunchy.

4 Remove and discard the lime leaf and stir in the basil leaves and coriander. Transfer to a warmed serving dish, garnish with peanuts and serve immediately.

Vegetable Cake

This is a savoury version of a cheesecake with a layer of fried potatoes as a delicious base. Use frozen mixed vegetables for the topping, if liked.

NUTRITIONAL INFORMATION

Calories 502	Sugars 8g
Protein 16g	Fat 31g
Carbohydrate ...41g	Saturates 14g

20 MINS   45 MINS

SERVES 4

INGREDIENTS

BASE

2 tbsp vegetable oil, plus extra for brushing

4 large waxy potatoes, thinly sliced

TOPPING

1 tbsp vegetable oil

1 leek, chopped

1 courgette, grated

1 red pepper, seeded and diced

1 green pepper, seeded and diced

1 carrot, grated

2 tsp chopped parsley

225 g/8 oz full-fat soft cheese

25 g/1 oz grated mature cheese

2 eggs, beaten

salt and pepper

shredded cooked leek, to garnish

salad, to serve

1 Brush a 20 cm/8 inch springform cake tin with oil.

2 To make the base, heat the oil in a frying pan. Cook the potato slices until softened and browned. Drain on kitchen paper and place in the base of the tin.

3 To make the topping, heat the oil in a separate frying pan. Add the leek and fry over a low heat, stirring frequently, for 3-4 minutes, until softened.

4 Add the courgette, peppers, carrot and parsley to the pan and cook over a low heat for 5-7 minutes, or until the vegetables have softened.

5 Meanwhile, beat the cheeses and eggs together in a bowl. Stir in the vegetables and season to taste with salt and pepper. Spoon the mixture evenly over the potato base.

6 Cook in a preheated oven, 190°C/ 375°F/Gas Mark 5, for 20-25 minutes, until the cake is set.

7 Remove the vegetable cake from the tin, transfer to a warm serving plate, garnish with shredded leek and serve with a crisp salad.

Vegetable Hot Pot

In this recipe, a variety of vegetables are cooked under a layer of potatoes, topped with cheese and cooked until golden brown.

NUTRITIONAL INFORMATION

Calories 279	Sugars 12g	
Protein 10g	Fat 11g	
Carbohydrate ...34g	Saturates 4g	

🥘 25 MINS   🕐 1 HOUR

SERVES 4

INGREDIENTS

2 large potatoes, thinly sliced

2 tbsp vegetable oil

1 red onion, halved and sliced

1 leek, sliced

2 garlic cloves, crushed

1 carrot, cut into chunks

100 g/3½ oz broccoli florets

100 g/3½ oz cauliflower florets

2 small turnips, quartered

1 tbsp plain flour

700 ml/1¼ pints vegetable stock

150 ml/¼ pint dry cider

1 eating apple, cored and sliced

2 tbsp chopped sage

pinch of cayenne pepper

50 g/1¾ oz grated Cheddar cheese

salt and pepper

1 Cook the potato slices in a saucepan of boiling water for 10 minutes. Drain thoroughly and reserve.

2 Heat the oil in a flameproof casserole. Add the onion, leek and garlic and sauté, stirring occasionally, for 2–3 minutes. Add the remaining vegetables and cook, stirring constantly, for a further 3–4 minutes.

3 Stir in the flour and cook for 1 minute. Gradually add the stock and cider and bring to the boil. Add the apple, sage and cayenne pepper and season well. Remove from the heat and transfer the vegetables to an ovenproof dish.

4 Arrange the potato slices on top of the vegetable mixture to cover.

5 Sprinkle the cheese on top of the potato slices and cook in a preheated oven, 190°C/375°F/Gas Mark 5, for 30–35 minutes or until the potato is golden brown and beginning to crispen around the edges. Serve immediately.

Lentil Roast

The perfect dish to serve for Sunday lunch. Roast vegetables make a succulent accompaniment.

NUTRITIONAL INFORMATION

Calories	 400	Sugars	.... 2g
Protein	.... 26g	Fat	.... 20g
Carbohydrate	... 32g	Saturates	...... 10g

15 MINS   1 HR 20 MINS

SERVES 6

I N G R E D I E N T S

225 g/8 oz red lentils

450 ml/16 fl oz vegetable stock

1 bay leaf

15 g/½ oz butter or margarine, softened

2 tbsp dried wholemeal breadcrumbs

225 g/8 oz grated mature Cheddar cheese

1 leek, finely chopped

125 g/4½ oz button mushrooms, finely chopped

90 g/3 oz fresh wholemeal breadcrumbs

2 tbsp chopped parsley

1 tbsp lemon juice

2 eggs, lightly beaten

salt and pepper

flat leaf parsley sprigs, to garnish

mixed roast vegetables, to serve

1 Put the lentils, stock and bay leaf in a saucepan. Bring to the boil, cover and simmer gently for 15–20 minutes, until all the liquid is absorbed and the lentils have softened. Discard the bay leaf.

2 Base-line a 1 kg/2 lb 4 oz loaf tin with baking parchment. Grease with the butter or margarine and sprinkle with the dried breadcrumbs.

3 Stir the cheese, leek, mushrooms, fresh breadcrumbs and parsley into the lentils.

4 Bind the mixture together with the lemon juice and eggs. Season with salt and pepper. Spoon into the prepared loaf tin and smooth the top.

5 Bake in a preheated oven, 190°C/ 375°F/Gas Mark 5, for about 1 hour, until golden.

6 Loosen the loaf with a palette knife and turn on to a warmed serving plate. Garnish with parsley and serve sliced, with roast vegetables.

Winter Vegetable Casserole

This hearty supper dish is best served with plenty of warm crusty bread to mop up the delicious juices.

NUTRITIONAL INFORMATION

Calories 211   Sugars 6g
Protein . . . . .11g   Fat 6g
Carbohydrate . . .26g   Saturates 0.8g

 10 MINS   40 MINS

SERVES 4

I N G R E D I E N T S

1 tbsp olive oil

1 red onion, halved and sliced

3 garlic cloves, crushed

225 g/8 oz spinach

1 fennel bulb, cut into eight

1 red pepper, seeded and cubed

1 tbsp plain flour

450 ml/16 fl oz vegetable stock

6 tbsp dry white wine

400 g/14 oz can chickpeas, drained

1 bay leaf

1 tsp ground coriander

½ tsp paprika

salt and pepper

fennel fronds, to garnish

1 Heat the olive oil in a large flameproof casserole. Add the onion and garlic and sauté over a low heat, stirring frequently, for 1 minute. Add the spinach and cook, stirring occasionally, for 4 minutes, or until wilted.

2 Add the fennel pieces and red pepper and cook, stirring constantly, for 2 minutes.

3 Stir in the flour and cook, stirring constantly, for 1 minute.

4 Add the vegetable stock, white wine, chickpeas, bay leaf, ground coriander and paprika, cover and simmer for 30 minutes. Season to taste with salt and pepper, garnish with fennel fronds and serve immediately straight from the casserole.

COOK'S TIP

Use other canned pulses or mixed beans instead of the chickpeas, if you prefer.

Cauliflower Bake

The red of the tomatoes is a great contrast to the cauliflower and herbs, making this dish appealing to both the eye and the palate.

NUTRITIONAL INFORMATION

Calories 305   Sugars 9g
Protein . . . . .15g   Fat 14g
Carbohydrate . . .31g   Saturates 6g

🥔 10 MINS   🕑 40 MINS

SERVES 4

INGREDIENTS

500 g/1 lb 2 oz cauliflower,
    broken into florets

2 large potatoes, cubed

100 g/3½ oz cherry tomatoes

SAUCE

25 g/1 oz butter or margarine

1 leek, sliced

1 garlic clove, crushed

25 g/1 oz plain flour

300 ml/½ pint milk

75 g/2¾ oz mixed grated cheese, such as
    Cheddar, Parmesan and Gruyère

½ tsp paprika

2 tbsp chopped flat leaf parsley

salt and pepper

chopped parsley, to garnish

VARIATION

This dish could be made with broccoli instead of the cauliflower as an alternative.

1 Cook the cauliflower in a saucepan of boiling water for 10 minutes. Drain well and reserve. Meanwhile, cook the potatoes in a pan of boiling water for 10 minutes, drain and reserve.

2 To make the sauce, melt the butter or margarine in a saucepan and sauté the leek and garlic for 1 minute. Stir in the flour and cook, stirring constantly, for 1 minute. Remove the pan from the heat and gradually stir in the milk, 50 g/ 1³/₄ oz of the cheese, the paprika and parsley. Return the pan to the heat and bring to the boil, stirring constantly. Season with salt and pepper to taste.

3 Spoon the cauliflower into a deep ovenproof dish. Add the cherry tomatoes and top with the potatoes. Pour the sauce over the potatoes and sprinkle on the remaining cheese.

4 Cook in a preheated oven, 180°C/ 350°F/Gas Mark 4, for 20 minutes, or until the vegetables are cooked through and the cheese is golden brown and bubbling. Garnish and serve immediately.

Lentil & Rice Casserole

This is a really hearty dish, perfect for cold days when a filling hot dish is just what you need.

NUTRITIONAL INFORMATION

Calories 312   Sugars 9g
Protein . . . . .20g   Fat 2g
Carbohydrate . . .51g   Saturates 0.4g

 15 MINS   40 MINS

SERVES 4

INGREDIENTS

225 g/8 oz split red lentils

50 g/1¾ oz long grain white rice

1.2 litres/2 pints vegetable stock

1 leek, cut into chunks

3 garlic cloves, crushed

400 g/14 oz can chopped tomatoes

1 tsp ground cumin

1 tsp chilli powder

1 tsp garam masala

1 red pepper, seeded and sliced

100 g/3½ oz small broccoli florets

8 baby corn cobs, halved lengthways

50 g/1¾ oz French beans, halved

1 tbsp shredded basil

salt and pepper

fresh basil sprigs, to garnish

1 Place the lentils, rice and vegetable stock in a large flameproof casserole and cook over a low heat, stirring occasionally, for 20 minutes.

2 Add the leek, garlic, tomatoes and their can juice, ground cumin, chilli powder, garam masala, sliced pepper, broccoli, corn cobs and French beans to the pan.

3 Bring the mixture to the boil, reduce the heat, cover and simmer for a further 10–15 minutes, or until the vegetables are tender.

4 Add the shredded basil and season with salt and pepper to taste.

5 Garnish with fresh basil sprigs and serve immediately.

VARIATION

You can vary the rice in this recipe – use brown or wild rice, if you prefer.

Tofu Skewers

Tofu is full of protein, vitamins and minerals and it develops a fabulous flavour when it is marinated in garlic and herbs.

NUTRITIONAL INFORMATION

Calories 149	Sugars 5g
Protein 13g	Fat 9g
Carbohydrate 5g	Saturates 1g

  45 MINS 15 MINS

SERVES 4

I N G R E D I E N T S

350 g/12 oz tofu

1 red pepper

1 yellow pepper

2 courgettes

8 button mushrooms

slices of lemon, to garnish

M A R I N A D E

grated rind and juice of ½ lemon

1 garlic clove, crushed

½ tsp rosemary, chopped

½ tsp chopped thyme

1 tbsp walnut oil

1 To make the marinade, combine the lemon rind and juice, garlic, rosemary, thyme and oil in a shallow dish.

2 Drain the tofu, pat it dry on kitchen paper and cut it into squares with a sharp knife. Add to the marinade and toss to coat thoroughly. Set aside to marinate for 20–30 minutes.

3 Meanwhile, seed the peppers and cut the flesh into 2.5 cm/1 inch pieces. Blanch in a saucepan of boiling water for 4 minutes, refresh in cold water and drain.

4 Using a canelle knife or swivel vegetable peeler, remove strips of peel from the courgettes. Cut the courgettes into 2.5 cm/1 inch chunks.

5 Remove the tofu from the marinade, reserving the marinade for basting. Thread the tofu on to 8 skewers, alternating with the peppers, courgette and button mushrooms.

6 Barbecue the skewers over medium hot coals for about 6 minutes, turning and basting with the marinade.

7 Transfer the skewers to serving plates, garnish with lemon slices and serve.

Tasty Barbecue Sauce

Just the thing for brushing on to vegetable kebabs and burgers, this sauce is easy and quick to make.

NUTRITIONAL INFORMATION

Calories	100	Sugars 9g
Protein	. . . . .1g	Fat 6g
Carbohydrate	. . .10g	Saturates 1g

 5 MINS   40 MINS

SERVES 4

I N G R E D I E N T S

25 g/1 oz butter or margarine

1 garlic clove, crushed

1 onion, finely chopped

400 g/14 oz can chopped tomatoes

1 tbsp dark muscovado sugar

1 tsp hot chilli sauce

1–2 gherkins

1 tbsp capers, drained

salt and pepper

1 Melt the butter or margarine in a saucepan and fry the garlic and onion for 8–10 minutes, until well browned.

2 Add the chopped tomatoes, sugar and chilli sauce. Bring to the boil, then reduce the heat and simmer gently for 20–25 minutes, until thick and pulpy.

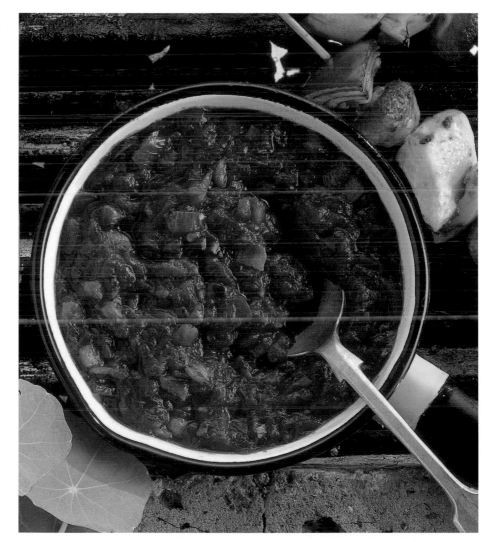

COOK'S TIP

To make sure that the sauce has a good colour, it is important to brown the onions really well to begin with. When fresh tomatoes are cheap and plentiful, they can be used instead of canned ones. Peel and chop 500 g/1 lb 2 oz.

3 Chop the gherkins and capers finely. Add to the sauce, stirring to mix. Cook the sauce over a low heat for 2 minutes.

4 Taste the sauce and season with a little salt and pepper to taste. Use as a baste for vegetarian kebabs and burgers, or as an accompaniment to other barbecued food.

Pumpkin Parcels with Chilli

This spicy side dish is perfect for a Hallowe'en or Bonfire Night barbecue party, although it is equally delicious on a summer evening, too.

NUTRITIONAL INFORMATION

Energy	118	Sugar	.........3g
Protein	.........1g	Fat	...........11g
Carbohydrates	....4g	Saturates	.......4g

 10 MINS   25-30 MINS

SERVES 4

INGREDIENTS

700 g/1 lb 9 oz pumpkin or squash

2 tbsp sunflower oil

25 g/1 oz butter

½ tsp chilli sauce

grated rind of 1 lime

2 tsp lime juice

1 Halve the pumpkin or squash and scoop out the seeds. Rinse the seeds and reserve. Cut the pumpkin into thin wedges and peel.

2 Heat the oil and butter together in a large saucepan, stirring constantly, until melted. Stir in the chilli sauce, lime rind and juice.

3 Add the pumpkin or squash and seeds to the pan and toss to coat all over in the flavoured butter.

4 Divide the mixture between 4 double thickness sheets of kitchen foil. Fold over the kitchen foil to enclose the pumpkin or squash mixture completely.

5 Barbecue the foil parcels over hot coals for 15–25 minutes, or until the pumpkin or squash is tender.

6 Transfer the foil parcels to warm serving plates. Open the parcels at the table and serve at once.

VARIATION

Add 2 teaspoons of curry paste to the oil instead of the lime and chilli. Use butternut squash when pumpkin is not available.

Turkish Kebabs

A spicy chickpea sauce is served with barbecued colourful vegetable kebabs.

NUTRITIONAL INFORMATION

Calories 303   Sugars 13g
Protein . . . . .13g   Fat 15g
Carbohydrate . . .30g   Saturates 2g

20 MINS   20 MINS

SERVES 4

INGREDIENTS

SAUCE

4 tbsp olive oil

3 garlic cloves, crushed

1 small onion, finely chopped

425 g/15 oz can chickpeas, rinsed and drained

300 ml/½ pint natural yogurt

1 tsp ground cumin

½ tsp chilli powder

lemon juice

salt and pepper

KEBABS

1 aubergine

1 red pepper, seeded

1 green pepper, seeded

4 plum tomatoes

1 lemon, cut into wedges

8 small fresh bay leaves

olive oil, for brushing

1 To make the sauce, heat the olive oil in a small frying pan. Add the garlic and onion and fry over a medium heat, stirring occasionally, for about 5 minutes, until the onion is softened and golden brown.

2 Put the chickpeas and yogurt into a blender or food processor and add the cumin, chilli powder and onion mixture. Process for about 15 seconds, until smooth. Alternatively, mash the chickpeas with a potato masher and stir in the yogurt, ground cumin, chilli powder and onion.

3 Place the puréed mixture in a bowl and season to taste with lemon juice, salt and pepper. Cover and chill until ready to serve.

4 To prepare the kebabs, cut the vegetables into large chunks and thread them on to 4 skewers, placing a bay leaf and lemon wedge at both ends of each kebab.

5 Brush the kebabs with olive oil and cook them over the barbecue, turning frequently, for 5–8 minutes. Heat the chickpea sauce and serve with the kebabs.

Citrus & Herb Marinades

Choose one of these marinades to give a marvellous flavour to barbecued food. The nutritional information is for Orange & Marjoram only.

NUTRITIONAL INFORMATION

Calories ....269 Sugars 3g
Protein ....0.4g Fat 6g
Carbohydrate ....3g Saturates 1g

 20 MINS   0 MINS

SERVES 4

INGREDIENTS

ORANGE & MARJORAM

1 orange

125 ml/4 fl oz olive oil

4 tbsp dry white wine

4 tbsp white wine vinegar

1 tbsp snipped chives

1 tbsp chopped marjoram

salt and pepper

THAI-SPICED LIME

1 lemon grass stalk

finely grated rind and juice of 1 lime

4 tbsp sesame oil

2 tbsp light soy sauce

pinch of ground ginger

1 tbsp chopped coriander

salt and pepper

BASIL & LEMON

finely grated rind of 1 lemon

4 tbsp lemon juice

1 tbsp balsamic vinegar

2 tbsp red wine vinegar

2 tbsp virgin olive oil

1 tbsp chopped oregano

1 tbsp chopped basil

salt and pepper

1 To make the Orange & Marjoram marinade, remove the rind from the orange with a zester, or grate it finely, then squeeze the juice.

2 Mix the orange rind and juice with all the remaining ingredients in a small bowl, whisking together to combine. Season with salt and pepper.

3 To make the Thai-Spiced Lime marinade, bruise the lemon grass by crushing it with a rolling pin. Mix the remaining ingredients together in a small bowl and add the lemon grass.

4 To make the Basil & Lemon marinade, whisk all the ingredients together in a small bowl. Season to taste with salt and pepper.

5 Keep the marinades covered with clear film or store them in screw-top jars, ready for using as marinades or bastes.

Sidekick Vegetables

Colourful vegetables are barbecued over hot coals to make this unusual hot salad, which is served with a spicy chilli sauce on the side.

NUTRITIONAL INFORMATION

Calories 224	Sugars 14g
Protein 4g	Fat 15g
Carbohydrate ...21g	Saturates 2g

15 MINS   30 MINS

SERVES 4

INGREDIENTS

1 red pepper, seeded

1 orange or yellow pepper, seeded

2 courgettes

2 corn cobs

1 aubergine

olive oil, for brushing

chopped thyme, rosemary and parsley

salt and pepper

lime or lemon wedges, to serve

DRESSING

2 tbsp olive oil

1 tbsp sesame oil

1 garlic clove, crushed

1 small onion, finely chopped

1 celery stick, finely chopped

1 small green chilli, seeded and chopped

4 tomatoes, chopped

5 cm/2 inch piece of cucumber, chopped

1 tbsp tomato purée

1 tbsp lime or lemon juice

1 To make the dressing, heat the olive and sesame oils together in a saucepan or frying pan. Add the garlic and onion, and fry over a low heat for about 3 minutes, until softened.

2 Add the celery, chilli and tomatoes to the pan and cook, stirring frequently, for 5 minutes.

3 Stir in the cucumber, tomato purée and lime or lemon juice, and simmer over a low heat for 8–10 minutes, until thick and pulpy. Season to taste with salt and pepper.

4 Cut the vegetables into thick slices and brush with a little olive oil.

5 Cook the vegetables over the hot coals of the barbecue for about 6–8 minutes, sprinkling them with salt and pepper and fresh herbs as they cook, and turning once.

6 Divide the vegetables between 4 serving plates and spoon some of the dressing on to the side. Serve at once, sprinkled with a few more chopped herbs and accompanied by the lime or lemon wedges.

Barbecued Bean Pot

Cook this tasty vegetable and Quorn casserole conventionally, then keep it piping hot over the barbecue.

NUTRITIONAL INFORMATION

Calories 381   Sugars 17g
Protein . . . . .21g   Fat 19g
Carbohydrate . . .34g   Saturates 3g

  10 MINS   1 HOUR

SERVES 4

I N G R E D I E N T S

60 g/2 oz butter or margarine

1 large onion, chopped

2 garlic cloves, crushed

2 carrots, sliced

2 celery sticks, sliced

1 tbsp paprika

2 tsp ground cumin

400 g/14 oz can of chopped tomatoes

425 g/15 oz can of mixed beans,
   rinsed and drained

150 ml/¼ pint vegetable stock

1 tbsp molasses sugar or black treacle

350 g/12 oz Quorn or soya cubes

salt and pepper

crusty French bread, to serve

VARIATION

If you prefer, cook the casserole in a preheated oven, 190°C/375°F/Gas Mark 5 from step 3, but keep the dish covered. Instead of mixed beans you could use just one type of canned beans.

1 Melt the butter or margarine in a large flameproof casserole and fry the onion and garlic over a medium heat, stirring occasionally, for about 5 minutes, until golden brown.

2 Add the carrots and celery and cook, stirring occasionally, for a further 2 minutes, then stir in the paprika and ground cumin.

3 Add the tomatoes and beans. Pour in the stock and add the sugar or treacle. Bring to the boil, then reduce the heat and

simmer, uncovered, stirring occasionally, for 30 minutes.

4 Add the Quorn or soya cubes to the casserole, cover and cook, stirring occasionally, for a further 20 minutes.

5 Season to taste, then transfer the casserole to the barbecue, setting it to one side to keep hot.

6 Ladle on to plates and serve with crusty French bread.

Hot Salad

This quickly-made dish is ideal for a cold winter's night.
Serve with crusty bread, freshly made rolls or garlic bread.

NUTRITIONAL INFORMATION

Calories	154	Sugars	........13g
Protein	.........4g	Fat	...........9g
Carbohydrate	...14g	Saturates	.......6g

 10 MINS 10 MINS

SERVES 4

I N G R E D I E N T S

½ medium-sized cauliflower

1 green pepper

1 red pepper

½ cucumber

4 carrots

2 tbsp butter

salt and pepper

crusty bread, rolls or garlic bread, to serve

D R E S S I N G

3 tbsp olive oil

1 tbsp white wine vinegar

1 tbsp light soy sauce

1 tsp caster sugar

salt and pepper

1 Cut the cauliflower into small florets, using a sharp knife. Seed the peppers and cut the flesh into thin slices. Cut the cucumber into thin slices. Thinly slice the carrots lengthways.

2 Melt the butter in a large heavy-based saucepan. Add the cauliflower florets, peppers, cucumber and carrots and fry over a medium heat, stirring constantly, for 5-7 minutes, until tender, but still firm to the bite. Season with salt and pepper. Lower the heat, cover with a lid, and simmer for 3 minutes.

3 Meanwhile, make the dressing. Whisk together all the ingredients until thoroughly combined.

4 Transfer the vegetables to a serving dish, pour over the dressing, toss to mix well and serve immediately.

VARIATION

You can replace the vegetables in this recipe with those of your choice, such as broccoli, spring onions and courgettes.

Alfalfa & Spinach Salad

This is a really refreshing salad that must be assembled just before serving to prevent everything being coloured by the beetroot.

NUTRITIONAL INFORMATION

Calories 139	Sugars 7g
Protein 2g	Fat 11g
Carbohydrate 8g	Saturates 2g

10 MINS   0 MINS

SERVES 4

INGREDIENTS

100 g/3½ oz baby spinach

75 g/2¾ oz alfalfa sprouts

2 celery sticks, sliced

4 cooked beetroot, cut into eight

DRESSING

4 tbsp olive oil

4½ tsp garlic wine vinegar

1 garlic clove, crushed

2 tsp clear honey

1 tbsp chopped chives

1 Place the spinach and alfalfa sprouts in a large bowl and mix together.

2 Add the celery to the bowl and mix together well.

3 Toss in the beetroot and mix until well combined.

4 To make the dressing, mix the oil, wine vinegar, garlic, honey and chopped chives.

5 Pour the dressing over the salad, toss well and serve immediately.

VARIATION

Add the segments of 1 large orange to the salad to make it even more colourful and refreshing. Replace the garlic wine vinegar with a different flavoured oil such as chilli or herb, if you prefer.

Moroccan Salad

Couscous is a type of semolina made from durum wheat. It is wonderful in salads, as it readily takes up the flavour of the dressing.

NUTRITIONAL INFORMATION

Calories	195	Sugars 15g
Protein	.........8g	Fat 2g
Carbohydrate	...40g	Saturates 0.3g

 30–35 MINS 0 MINS

SERVES 6

INGREDIENTS

175 g/6 oz couscous

1 bunch spring onions, finely chopped

1 small green pepper, seeded and chopped

10 cm/4 inch piece of cucumber, chopped

175 g/6 oz can chickpeas,
    rinsed and drained

60 g/2 oz sultanas or raisins

2 oranges

salt and pepper

mint sprigs, to garnish

lettuce leaves, to serve

DRESSING

finely grated rind of 1 orange

1 tbsp chopped fresh mint

150 ml/¼ pint natural yogurt

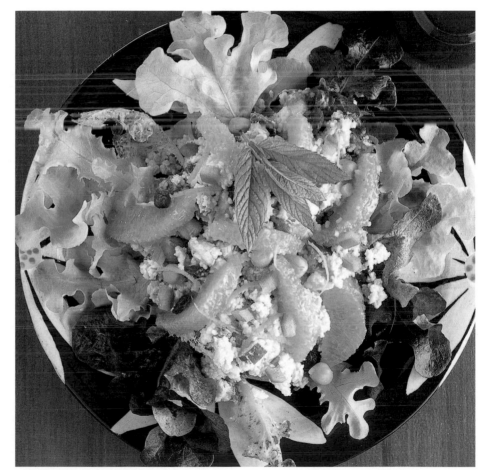

1 Put the couscous into a bowl and cover with boiling water. Leave it to soak for about 15 minutes to swell the grains, then stir gently with a fork to separate them.

2 Add the spring onions, green pepper, cucumber, chickpeas and sultanas or raisins to the couscous, stirring to combine. Season well with salt and pepper.

3 To make the dressing, place the orange rind, mint and yogurt in a bowl and mix together until well combined. Pour over the couscous mixture and stir to mix well.

4 Using a sharp serrated knife, remove the peel and pith from the oranges. Cut the flesh into segments, removing all the membrane.

5 Arrange the lettuce leaves on 4 serving plates. Divide the couscous mixture between the plates and arrange the orange segments on top. Garnish with sprigs of fresh mint and serve.

Marinated Vegetable Salad

Lightly steamed vegetables taste superb served slightly warm in a marinade of olive oil, white wine, vinegar and fresh herbs.

NUTRITIONAL INFORMATION

Calories 114	Sugars 4g	
Protein 3g	Fat 9g	
Carbohydrate 5g	Saturates 1g	

 10 MINS   🕐 10 MINS

SERVES 6

I N G R E D I E N T S

175 g/6 oz baby carrots

2 celery hearts, cut into 4 pieces

125g/4½ oz sugar snap peas or mangetout

1 fennel bulb, sliced

175 g/6 oz small asparagus spears

1½ tbsp sunflower seeds

dill sprigs, to garnish

D R E S S I N G

4 tbsp olive oil

4 tbsp dry white wine

2 tbsp white wine vinegar

1 tbsp chopped dill

1 tbsp chopped parsley

salt and pepper

1 Put the carrots, celery, sugar snap peas or mangetout, fennel and asparagus into a steamer and cook over gently boiling water until just tender. It is important that they retain a little 'bite'.

2 Meanwhile, make the dressing. Mix together the olive oil, wine, vinegar and chopped herbs, whisking until thoroughly combined. Season to taste with salt and pepper.

3 When the vegetables are cooked, transfer them to a serving dish and pour over the dressing at once. The hot vegetables will absorb the flavour of the dressing as they cool.

4 Spread out the sunflower seeds on a baking tray and toast them under a preheated grill for 3-4 minutes or until lightly browned. Sprinkle the toasted sunflower seeds over the vegetables.

5 Serve the salad while the vegetables are still slightly warm, garnished with sprigs of fresh dill.

Warm Goat's Cheese Salad

This delicious salad combines soft goat's cheese with walnut halves, served on a bed of mixed salad leaves.

NUTRITIONAL INFORMATION

Calories 408	Sugars 8g	
Protein 9g	Fat 38g	
Carbohydrate 8g	Saturates 8g	

 5 MINS   🕐 5 MINS

SERVES 4

I N G R E D I E N T S

90 g/3 oz/¾ cup walnut halves

mixed salad leaves (greens)

125 g/4½ oz soft goat's cheese

snipped chives, to garnish

D R E S S I N G

6 tbsp walnut oil

3 tbsp white wine vinegar

1 tbsp clear honey

1 tsp Dijon mustard

pinch of ground ginger

salt and pepper

VARIATION

You could also use a ewe's milk cheese, such as feta, in this recipe for a sharper flavour.

1 To make the dressing, whisk together the walnut oil, wine vinegar, honey, mustard and ginger in a small saucepan. Season to taste with salt and pepper.

2 Heat the dressing gently, stirring occasionally, until warm. Add the walnut halves and continue to heat for 3–4 minutes.

3 Arrange the salad leaves on 4 serving plates and place spoonfuls of goat's cheese on top. Lift the walnut halves from the dressing with a slotted spoon, and scatter them over the salads.

4 Transfer the warm dressing to a small jug. Sprinkle chives over the salads and serve with the dressing.

Multicoloured Salad

The beetroot adds a rich colour to this dish, tinting the potato an appealing pink. Mixed with cucumber it is a really vibrant salad.

NUTRITIONAL INFORMATION

Calories	174	Sugars	.........8g
Protein	.........4g	Fat	..........6g
Carbohydrate	...27g	Saturates	.......1g

 15-20 MINS   20 MINS

SERVES 4

I N G R E D I E N T S

500 g/1 lb 2 oz waxy potatoes, diced

4 small cooked beetroot, sliced

½ small cucumber, thinly sliced

2 large dill pickles, sliced

1 red onion, halved and sliced

dill sprigs, to garnish

D R E S S I N G

1 garlic clove, crushed

2 tbsp olive oil

2 tbsp red wine vinegar

2 tbsp chopped fresh dill

salt and pepper

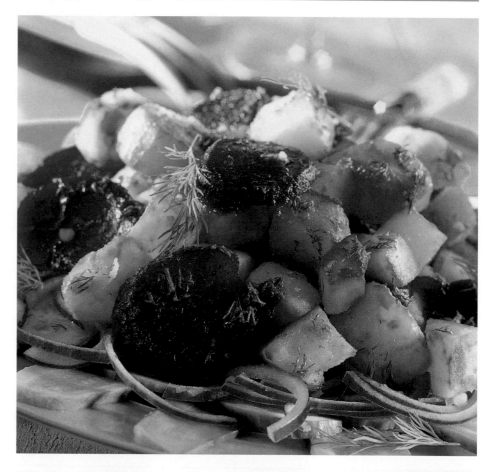

1 Cook the diced potatoes in a saucepan of boiling water for about 15 minutes, or until just tender. Drain and set aside to cool.

2 When cool, mix the potato and beetroot together in a bowl and set aside.

3 To make the dressing, whisk together the garlic, olive oil, vinegar and dill and season to taste with salt and pepper.

4 When ready to serve, line a large serving platter with the slices of cucumber, dill pickles and red onion. Spoon the potato and beetroot mixture into the centre of the platter.

5 Pour the dressing over the salad and serve immediately, garnished with fresh dill sprigs.

VARIATION

Line the salad platter with 2 heads of chicory, separated into leaves, and arrange the cucumber, dill pickle and red onion slices on top of the leaves.

Middle Eastern Salad

This attractive-looking salad can be served with a couple of vegetable kebabs for a delicious light lunch or an informal supper.

NUTRITIONAL INFORMATION

Calories 163   Sugars 12g
Protein ....8g   Fat 3g
Carbohydrate ...27g   Saturates 0.4g

15 MINS   0 MINS

SERVES 4

I N G R E D I E N T S

400 g/14 oz can chickpeas

4 carrots

1 bunch spring onions

1 medium cucumber

½ tsp salt

½ tsp pepper

3 tbsp lemon juice

1 red pepper, sliced

1 Drain the chickpeas and place them in a large salad bowl.

2 Using a sharp knife, thinly slice the carrots. Cut the spring onions into small pieces. Thickly slice the cucumber and then cut the slices into quarters.

3 Add the carrot slices, spring onions and cucumber to the chickpeas and mix.

4 Season to taste with the salt and pepper and sprinkle with the lemon juice. Toss the salad ingredients together gently, using 2 serving spoons.

5 Using a sharp knife, thinly slice the red pepper. Arrange the slices of red pepper decoratively on top of the

chickpea salad. Serve the salad immediately or chill in the refrigerator and serve when required.

VARIATION

This salad would also be delicious made with *ful medames*. If they are not available canned, use 150g/5½ oz dried, soaked for 5 hours and then simmered for 2½ hours. Another alternative would be canned gunga beans.

Kashmiri Spinach

This is an imaginative way to serve spinach, which adds a little zip to it. It is a very simple dish, which will complement almost any curry.

NUTRITIONAL INFORMATION

Calories 81	Sugars 2g
Protein 4g	Fat 7g
Carbohydrate 2g	Saturates 1g

🕭 5 MINS   🕙 25 MINS

SERVES 4

INGREDIENTS

500 g/1 lb 2 oz spinach or Swiss chard or baby leaf spinach

2 tbsp mustard oil

¼ tsp garam masala

1 tsp yellow mustard seeds

2 spring onions, sliced

1 Remove the tough stalks from the spinach.

2 Heat the mustard oil in a preheated wok or large heavy-based frying pan until it smokes. Add the garam masala and mustard seeds. Cover the pan quickly – you will hear the mustard seeds popping inside.

3 When the popping has ceased, remove the cover, add the spring onions and spinach. Cook, stirring constantly, until the spinach has wilted.

4 Continue cooking the spinach, uncovered, over a medium heat for 10–15 minutes, until most of the water has evaporated. If using frozen spinach, it will not need to cook for so long – cook it until most of the water has evaporated.

5 Remove the spinach and spring onions with a slotted spoon, draining off any

remaining liquid. (This dish is pleasanter to eat when it is served as dry as possible.)

6 Transfer to a warmed serving dish and serve immediately, while it is still piping hot.

COOK'S TIP

Mustard oil is made from mustard seeds and is very fiery when raw. However, when it is heated to this smoking stage, it loses a lot of the fire and takes on a delightful sweet quality.

Long Beans with Tomatoes

Indian meals often need some green vegetables to complement the spicy dishes and to set off the rich sauces.

NUTRITIONAL INFORMATION

Calories 76   Sugars 3g
Protein ....2g   Fat 6g
Carbohydrate ....4g   Saturates 3g

15 MINS   25 MINS

SERVES 6

INGREDIENTS

500 g/1 lb 2 oz green beans, cut into
    5 cm/2 inch lengths

2 tbsp vegetable ghee

2.5 cm/1 inch piece of root ginger, grated

1 garlic clove, crushed

1 tsp turmeric

½ tsp cayenne

1 tsp ground coriander

4 tomatoes, peeled, seeded and diced

150 ml/¼ pint vegetable stock

1 Blanch the beans briefly in boiling water, drain, refresh under cold running water and drain again.

2 Melt the ghee in a large saucepan over a moderate heat. Add the grated ginger and crushed garlic, stir and add the turmeric, cayenne and ground coriander. Stir over a low heat for about 1 minute, until fragrant.

3 Add the diced tomatoes, tossing them until they are thoroughly coated in the spice mix.

4 Add the vegetable stock to the pan, bring to the boil and cook over a medium-high heat, stirring occasionally, for about 10 minutes, until the sauce has thickened.

5 Add the beans, reduce the heat to moderate and heat through, stirring constantly, for 5 minutes.

6 Transfer to a warmed serving dish and serve immediately.

COOK'S TIP

Ginger graters are an invaluable piece of equipment to have when cooking Indian food. These small flat graters, made of either bamboo or china, can be held directly over the pan while you grate.

Broccoli with Fluffy Eggs

Broccoli or cauliflower florets in a mustard sauce are topped with an egg yolk set in whisked egg white and finished off with grated cheese.

NUTRITIONAL INFORMATION

Calories	733	Sugars	........11g
Protein	........43g	Fat	..........53g
Carbohydrate	...23g	Saturates	......25g

10 MINS   15 MINS

SERVES 1

INGREDIENTS

175 g/6 oz broccoli or cauliflower florets

15 g/½ oz butter or margarine

15 g/½ oz flour

150 ml/¼ pint milk

1 tbsp coarse grain mustard

dash of lemon juice

90 g/3 oz grated mature Cheddar cheese

1 large egg, separated

salt and pepper

paprika, to garnish

1 Cook the broccoli or cauliflower in boiling lightly salted water for about 3–4 minutes, until tender, but still crisp.

2 Meanwhile, melt the butter or margarine in a small saucepan. Stir in the flour and cook, stirring constantly, for 1 minute. Gradually add the milk and bring to the boil, stirring constantly until thickened. Season to taste with salt and pepper. Stir in the mustard and lemon juice and simmer for 1–2 minutes.

3 Remove the sauce from the heat and stir in two-thirds of the grated cheese until melted.

4 Drain the broccoli or cauliflower very thoroughly and place on an ovenproof plate or dish. Pour the cheese sauce over the vegetables.

5 Whisk the egg white until very stiff and season lightly. Pile the egg white on top of the broccoli or cauliflower and make a well in the centre.

6 Drop the egg yolk into the well in the egg white and sprinkle with the remaining cheese. Place under a preheated moderate grill for 3–4 minutes, until the meringue is lightly browned and the cheese has melted. Serve immediately, sprinkled with paprika.

Baby Cauliflowers

Whole baby cauliflowers coated with a red Leicester cheese and poppy seed sauce are cooked to perfection in the microwave oven.

NUTRITIONAL INFORMATION

Calories	173	Sugars	........6g
Protein	........8g	Fat	..........11g
Carbohydrate	...10g	Saturates	.......6g

🍲 30 MINS   🕐 15 MINS

SERVES 4

I N G R E D I E N T S

4 cloves

½ onion

½ carrot

1 bouquet garni

250 ml/9 fl oz milk

4 baby cauliflowers

3 tbsp water

15 g/½ oz butter

15 g/½ oz plain flour

60 g/2 oz grated red Leicester cheese

1 tbsp poppy seeds

pinch of paprika

salt and pepper

parsley, to garnish

1 Stick the cloves into the onion. Place in a bowl with the carrot, bouquet garni and milk. Heat on HIGH power for 2½–3 minutes. Leave to stand for 20 minutes to allow the flavours to infuse.

2 Trim the base and leaves from the cauliflowers and scoop out the stem using a small sharp knife, leaving the cauliflowers intact. Place the cauliflowers upside down in a large dish. Add the water, cover and cook on HIGH power for 5 minutes, until just tender. Leave to stand for 2–3 minutes.

3 Put the butter in a bowl and cook on HIGH power for 30 seconds, until melted. Stir in the flour. Cook on HIGH power for 30 seconds.

4 Strain the milk into a jug, discarding the vegetables. Gradually add to the flour and butter, beating well between each addition. Cover and cook on HIGH power for 3 minutes, stirring every 30 seconds after the first minute, until the sauce has thickened.

5 Stir the cheese and poppy seeds into the sauce and season with salt and pepper to taste. Cover and cook on HIGH power for 30 seconds.

6 Drain the cauliflowers and arrange on a plate or in a shallow dish. Pour over the sauce and sprinkle with a little paprika. Cook on HIGH power for 1 minute to reheat. Serve garnished with fresh parsley.

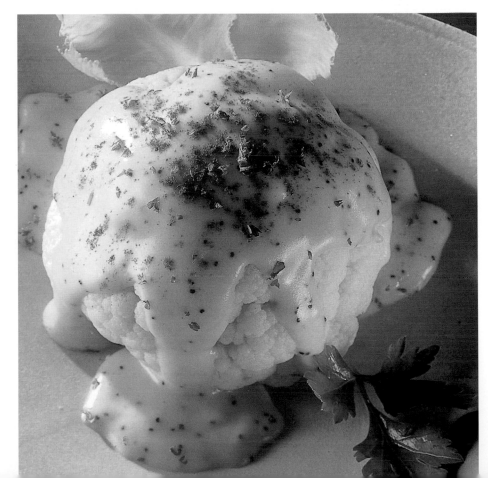

Baked Celery with Cream

This dish is topped with breadcrumbs for a crunchy topping, underneath which is hidden a creamy celery and pecan mixture.

NUTRITIONAL INFORMATION

Calories 237   Sugars 5g
Protein . . . . .7g   Fat 19g
Carbohydrate . . . .11g   Saturates 7g

 15 MINS   40 MINS

SERVES 4

I N G R E D I E N T S

1 head of celery

½ tsp ground cumin

½ tsp ground coriander

1 garlic clove, crushed

1 red onion, thinly sliced

50 g/1¾ oz pecan nut halves

150 ml/¼ pint vegetable stock

150 ml/¼ pint single cream

50 g/1¾ oz fresh wholemeal breadcrumbs

25 g/1 oz grated Parmesan cheese

salt and pepper

celery leaves, to garnish

COOK'S TIP

Once grated, Parmesan cheese quickly loses its 'bite' so it is best to grate only the amount you need for the recipe. Wrap the rest tightly in foil and it will keep for several months in the refrigerator.

1 Trim the celery and cut into matchsticks. Place the celery in an ovenproof dish, together with the ground cumin, coriander, garlic, red onion and pecan nuts.

2 Mix the stock and cream together and pour over the vegetables. Season with salt and pepper to taste.

3 Mix the breadcrumbs and cheese together and sprinkle over the top to cover the vegetables.

4 Cook in a preheated oven, 200°C/400°F/Gas Mark 6, for 40 minutes, or until the vegetables are tender and the top crispy. Garnish with celery leaves and serve at once.

Courgette Curry

This delicious curry is spiced with fenugreek seeds, which have a beautiful aroma and a distinctive taste.

NUTRITIONAL INFORMATION

Calories	188	Sugars	.........5g
Protein	.........3g	Fat	..........17g
Carbohydrate	....6g	Saturates	.......2g

20 MINS   15 MINS

SERVES 4

INGREDIENTS

6 tbsp vegetable oil

1 medium onion, finely chopped

3 fresh green chillies, finely chopped

1 tsp finely chopped root ginger

1 tsp crushed garlic

1 tsp chilli powder

500 g/1 lb 2 oz courgettes, thinly sliced

2 tomatoes, sliced

fresh coriander leaves, plus extra to garnish

2 tsp fenugreek seeds

chapatis, to serve

1 Heat the oil in a large, heavy-based frying pan.

2 Add the onion, fresh green chillies, ginger, garlic and chilli powder to the pan, stirring well to combine.

3 Add the sliced courgettes and the sliced tomatoes to the pan and stir-fry over a medium heat, for 5-7 minutes.

4 Add the cilantro leaves and fenugreek seeds to the courgette mixture in the pan and stir-fry over a medium heat for 5 minutes, until the vegetables are tender.

5 Remove the pan from the heat and transfer the courgette and fenugreek seed mixture to serving dishes. Garnish and serve hot with chapatis.

VARIATION

You could use coriander seeds instead of the fenugreek seeds, if you prefer.

Rice & Banana Brûlée

Take a can of rice pudding, flavour it with orange rind, stem ginger, raisins and sliced bananas and top with a brown sugar glaze.

NUTRITIONAL INFORMATION

Calories 509	Sugars 98g	
Protein 9g	Fat 6g	
Carbohydrate . . .112g	Saturates 4g	

5 MINS   5 MINS

SERVES 2

INGREDIENTS

400 g/14 oz can creamed rice pudding

grated rind of ½ orange

2 pieces stem ginger, finely chopped

2 tsp ginger syrup from the jar

40 g/1½ oz raisins

1–2 bananas

1–2 tsp lemon juice

4–5 tbsp demerara sugar

1 Empty the can of rice pudding into a bowl and mix in the grated orange rind, ginger, ginger syrup and raisins.

2 Cut the bananas diagonally into slices, toss in the lemon juice to prevent them from discolouring, drain and divide between 2 individual flameproof dishes.

3 Spoon the rice mixture in an even layer over the bananas so the dishes are almost full.

4 Sprinkle an even layer of sugar over the rice in each dish.

5 Place the dishes under a preheated moderate grill and heat until the sugar melts, taking care the sugar does not burn.

6 Set aside to cool until the caramel sets, then chill in the refrigerator until ready to serve. Tap the caramel with the back of a spoon to break it.

COOK'S TIP

Canned rice pudding is very versatile and is delicious heated with orange segments and grated apples added. Try it served cold with grated chocolate and mixed chopped nuts stirred through it.

Butterscotch Melts

This delicious dessert will go down a treat with children of all ages. Bananas and marshmallows taste fantastic with butterscotch sauce.

NUTRITIONAL INFORMATION

Calories	385	Sugar	........67g
Protein	.........2g	Fat	..........13g
Carbohydrate	...70g	Saturates	.......8g

 5 MINS 5 MINS

SERVES 4

I N G R E D I E N T S

4 bananas

4 tbsp lemon juice

225 g/8 oz marshmallows

S A U C E

125 g/4½ oz butter

125 g/4½ oz light muscovado sugar

125 g/4½ oz golden syrup

4 tbsp hot water

1 Slice the bananas into large chunks and dip them into the lemon juice to prevent them from going brown.

2 Thread the marshmallows and pieces of banana alternately on to kebab sticks or bamboo skewers, placing 2 marshmallows and 1 piece of banana on to each one.

COOK'S TIP

The warm butterscotch sauce tastes wonderful with vanilla ice cream. Make double the quantity of sauce if you plan to serve ice cream at a barbecue. Ideally, prepare the kebabs just before they are cooked to prevent the bananas from turning brown.

3 To make the sauce, melt the butter, sugar and syrup together in a small saucepan. Add the hot water, stirring until blended and smooth. Do not boil or else the mixture will become toffee-like. Keep the sauce warm at the edge of the barbecue, stirring from time to time.

4 Sear the kebabs over the barbecue coals for 30–40 seconds, turning constantly, so that the marshmallows are just beginning to brown and melt.

5 Serve the kebabs with a little of the butterscotch sauce spooned over them. (Use half of the sauce to serve 4; the remainder can be used later.)

This is a Parragon Book
This edition published in 2004

Parragon
Queen Street House
4 Queen Street
Bath BA1 1HE, UK

ISBN 1-40543-896-7

Printed in China

With grateful thanks to Claire Dashwood.

Material in this book has previously appeared in Ultimate Recipes Low Fat, Ultimate Recipes Vegetarian, Ultimate Recipes Italian, Ultimate Recipes Chinese, originally produced by Haldane Mason, London.

Notes
Use all metric or all imperial quantities, as the two are not interchangeable. Cup measurements in this book are for American cups. Tablespoons are assumed to be 15 ml. Unless otherwise stated, milk is assumed to be full fat, eggs are medium and pepper is freshly ground black pepper.

The nutritional information provided for each recipe is per serving or per portion. Optional ingredients, variations or serving suggestions have not been included in the calculations. The times given for each recipe are an approximate guide only as the preparation times may differ as a result of the type of oven used.